Francis Howard Williams

**A Reformer in ruffles**

A Comedy in three Acts

Francis Howard Williams

**A Reformer in ruffles**
*A Comedy in three Acts*

ISBN/EAN: 9783337055004

Printed in Europe, USA, Canada, Australia, Japan

Cover: Foto ©ninafisch / pixelio.de

More available books at **www.hansebooks.com**

# A REFORMER IN RUFFLES.

## 𝔄 Comedy

## IN THREE ACTS.

Scene. NEAR LONDON.
Costumes. XVIIIth CENTURY—POWDERED WIGS.

PUBLISHED FOR THE AUTHOR

# A REFORMER IN RUFFLES.

## A COMEDY IN THREE ACTS.

·  ———— — —

### DRAMATIS PERSONÆ.

COUNTESS OF TOUCHSTONE,—*In the inner circle of the Societary Beatitudes.*

HELENA RENAISSANCE,— *Her Daughter.* " *Really most quaintly sweet.*"

SAPPHO ARABESQUE,—*Niece to the Countess.* "*Quite chastely mediæval.*"

LADY IRONSIDES, *D.C.L. Oxon., Ph.D.*

LORD TOUCHSTONE-PEPPER, *Fifth Earl of Touchstone,—who "doesn't like contradiction, you know.*"

LORD DE PORTMENT,—*who esteems a graceful carriage above much riches.*

SIR HARRY SANGFROID,—*Lineal descendant of Sir Q. Cumber, Bart.*

SIR MEEKLY IRONSIDES,—*Fourth Assistant Secretary to the Woman Suffrage Association.*

BOGGS.

## ACT FIRST.

SCENE.— *Garden adjoining the country residence of the Earl of Touchstone. Double gate, centre, opening to park beyond. Wall at back with spiked coping. Flower-beds each side of gateway. Mansion at left, with doorway and steps to garden. Flower-beds and shrubbery at left, back. Flower stand with potted roses. Grass-plot at right. Rustic bench, small rustic table, and two chairs, right.—Time, the forenoon.*

(*The Countess of Touchstone and Lady Helena discovered seated at the table.*)

COUNTESS. How absurd of you, Helena. The man isn't of

our set, I tell you.   How, then, *can* he have an "Olympic head"?

HELENA.   But, sweet mamma, his pose is really most restful.   Quite Corinthian in fact.   And his brow—ah! (*sighs.*)

COUNTESS.   Nonsense, Helena.   His brow *can't* be fine, it's absolutely impossible.   Why, his grandfather was only a baronet!

HELENA.   That's all Sir Harry is now, mamma.

COUNTESS.   Ah, but Sir Harry's of our set.   And then Sir Harry is a young man yet, full of ardor and every manly virtue.   His great-granduncle's maternal grandfather was knighted by James I. for his services in suppressing the tobacco traffic.   Blue blood, Helena, blue blood through nine generations.   Why wasn't his mother a Fitz Gobble,—a junior branch of the Gobbles of Gobbleton?   And doesn't his tree show a straight line back to Sir Q. Cumber, who, on the field of Bosworth, when Earl Richmond had the tip of his nose carried away by an arrow, deliberately snipped off a piece of his own organ of scent and bound it to the Earl's face, so that the royal house of Tudor should not come to the throne noseless?

Blood will tell, Helena.   And Sir Harry's a gentleman.

HELENA.   But, sweet mamma, methinks Sir Harry is less chastely statuesque than Lord de Portment.

COUNTESS.   Lord de Portment!   I tell you, my dear, he isn't of our set, and I really couldn't think of your receiving the attentions of any one outside.   Why Lord de Portment actually goes to Lady Boodle's soirées.   Think of it!   And the Boodles were in trade thirty years ago.   Booh!

HELENA.   Ah dear!   The ideal counts for little in this soulless world.   One yearns with a sorrowful longing—a sort of painful solicitude—at times.   And they say Sir Harry is very reckless at gaming, mamma.

COUNTESS.   Tut, tut.   He must have his fling, to be sure.   It's aristocratic to play high.   It is only the parvenues who reckon up their bank accounts before making their stakes.   Sir Harry has the lavish hand of the old *noblesse.*   Now, can you for a moment imagine de Portment playing for heavy stakes?   de Portment, with his vulgar attempts at attitudinizing and his sham graces!   Ha, ha, ha.   It's preposterous!   Ha, ha, ha.

HELENA.   Oh, do please laugh in a minor key, sweet mamma.   You really jar my aural sense of the beautiful.   Dear Lady Sappho says there should always be a certain sense of the soul's anguish in a laugh—an echo of the pain of life in fact. Laughs in the major key went out with Titian.

COUNTESS. Helena, I have no objection to your indulging your taste for mediæval study, but don't attempt to instruct me in etiquette, if you please. Knowledge of how to laugh, when to laugh, and what to laugh at, is a prerequisite to admission to the inner circles of society. I consider Lord de Portment a very proper object of merriment, I assure you. And I beg that you will not let me hear of his foolish suit again.

HELENA. Oh, dear. Alas! he is *so* statuesque! And, sweet mamma, they say he never bores one by being much at home. He almost *lives* at his club. Ah— (*sighing.*)

COUNTESS. Now, don't grow melancholy, Helena. You know the Ironsides will be here for a fortnight, and I want you to be as lively as possible. Besides, you will have Sappho with you. Is she taking a rest after her long ride?

HELENA. Yes. I left the dear girl in her boudoir. She will be down as soon as she removes her travel stains. What a pity we can't travel by some aerial arrangement of wings, isn't it? The thought of a coach is so abhorrent to one's calm!

COUNTESS. My dear child, you should really get your nerves into better training. We can scarcely live on rose-leaves, and you know how irascible your papa is, and how affectation annoys him.

HELENA. Affectation! Ah, no; only refinement, mamma. I do wish dear papa were not quite so *modern* in his temper. If he would only base his rage on Greek models! *Herculean* anger would be sublime.

(*Enter from house, Boggs.*)

BOGGS. My Lady H'ironsides, my Lady. H'also, Sir Meekly H'ironsides, my Lady.

COUNTESS (*tossing embroidery to Helena.*) There, Helena, do be engaged upon something elegant. Embroidering that moss rose, for instance.

HELENA (*leaning back languidly.*) Thanks, sweet mamma, but methinks an ideal languor becomes me better.

(*Enter from house, Lady Ironsides, followed by Sir Meekly.*)

COUNTESS (*meeting them.*) So glad you came to the garden, dear Lady Ironsides. Sir Meekly, I trust you feel refreshed.

1*

Lady I. Thanks. He does. He had an excellent night's rest. (*To Sir M.*) Sit over there, Sir Meekly.

Sir M. Y' y' y'es, my love.

Lady I. What a charming spot, Countess. How much you must revel in these flowers! (*aside.*) A mean little pen to be called a garden.

Countess. Oh, pleasant for a month's rest, you know. London wears on one so towards the close of the season.

(*Sir M. mistakes a stand of roses for a rustic chair, and in trying to seat himself tumbles headlong into the flower-bed.*)

Lady I. Good heavens! Sir Meekly. Haven't you eyes?

Sir M. (*from flower-bed.*) Y' y' yes, my love. That is— I think . . .

Lady I. Well, you *shouldn't* think. Look! Why don't you look? (*Boggs assists Sir M. to rise.*)

Countess. I trust you are not hurt.

Helena (*aside.*) So unpleasantly precipitate.

Lady I. The fact is, Lady Touchstone, he has been a trifle near-sighted ever since Mrs. Amadeus Hector delivered her sublime oration on the Woman of the Future. Being fourth assistant secretary to the Suffrage Association, it became Sir Meekly's duty to copy out that oration for the press. He complained of his eyes at the 418th page . . .

Countess. Good gracious!

Lady I. Yes, poor man. But in such a noble cause, you know.

Helena. By my troth, methinks the task were all too hard.

Lady I. (*aside.*) What a fool that girl is.

Countess. Boggs, get a whisk and brush Sir Meekly off.

(*Exit Boggs.*)

Sir M. Th' th' thanks, very much I f' fear I've crushed your p' p' pansies.

Countess. Don't speak of it.

Sir M. (*pulling flowers from his ear.*) There are t' two pansies in my left e' ear.

(*Re-enter Boggs with whisks. He brushes Sir M.'s coat.*)

Countess. I believe you are quite interested in the rights of woman, my Lady?

Lady I. 'Tis the objective point of my existence. Thanks to such women as Mrs. Amadeus Hector, victory is now within our grasp. The next session of Parliament is sure to give us justice.

(*Exit Boggs, L.*)

Countess. Is Mrs. Hector in—in *society*, you know?

Lady I. A woman quite independent of society ; indeed quite above *sex*.

Helena. Spirit of Aphrodite ! How very dreadful.

Lady I. (*aside*.) I knew she was a fool.

Countess. Spare your comments, Helena. Pray proceed, my Lady. You think Parliament is going to legislate in favor of . . .

Lady I. In favor of woman's liberation. Should I have the pleasure of driving down to this delightful seat next season, I expect to come attended by a coach-woman, and a foot-woman, and ' . . .

Sir M. And to be received b' by your f' flunkeyess, my L' Lady.

Lady I. Sir Meekly !

Sir M. Y' y' yes, my love.

Helena. On my faith, an' I be not deceived, 'tis but a limping ambition !

Sir M. N' no, my dear young lady. T' 'tis g' grand ! Woman is bound to be a f' flunkeyess, before she g' gets through.

Lady I. Meekly, you talk so incessantly ! Be good enough to permit others to express an *occasional* opinion.

Sir M. Y' y' yes, my love.

Countess. Ha, ha ! I hope you may not find the rights of woman synonymous with her degradation.

Helena (*springing up*.) Ah, joy ! There is dear Sappho.

(*Enter from house, Lady Sappho. Sappho and Helena embrace rapturously in centre of stage.*)

Countess. My Lady Ironsides, permit me to present to you my niece, the Lady Sappho Arabesque. Sappho, Sir Meekly Ironsides.

Sappho. So glad.

Lady I. Ah, I suppose you find this lovely retreat quite captivating, my dear young lady ? Do you read much ?

SAPPHO. Really, I, aw, hardly know, you know. My heart's sister can answer better than I. (*To Helena.*) Do we read much, sweet?

HELENA. Oh, so much! Roundels from the early French mostly; such quaint, quaint bits.

SAPPHO. Ah! so full of soul.

LADY I. (*aside.*) A worse fool than the other! (*To Sappho.*) Did you ever read " Mrs. Bloodkins on Female Vengeance"?

(*Sappho screams.*)

HELENA. Olympian Zens!

COUNTESS. I suspect they rarely indulge in *heary* reading, my Lady.

LADY I. Heavy! What can be lighter than the brain-work of such women as Mrs. Bloodkins?

(*Sir Meekly, in wandering about, at back, has caught his stock in one of the spikes on top of the garden wall, and is wriggling, half suspended and choking.*)

SIR M. Ow—wow—fitz—ow.

COUNTESS. Oh, dear. He is caught on one of the spikes. Boggs, Boggs.

(*Enter, hurriedly, Boggs, L.*)

LADY I. (*calmly.*) Unhook him. Take him down.

BOGGS (*assisting Sir M.*) H'any dislocation, sir!

SIR M. N—no! thanks very much. I—I really was I—looking for . . .

(*Exit Boggs.*)

LADY I. Well, you *shouldn't* look. Think! Why don't you think? The fact is, Lady Touchstone, Sir Meekly is afflicted with chronic weakness in the left knee . . .

(*Helena and Sappho scream.*)

LADY I. Good heavens! young ladies; what *is* the matter?

SAPPHO. Greek art doesn't admit of any knee, madam, and . . .

HELENA. A true mediaevalism demands but a single curve from torso to ankle. (*To Sappho.*) To think of it, sweet, a knee . . Boo-oh!

SAPPHO. Boo–oh? Horrible! Ah . . .

COUNTESS. My Lady, you must pardon a slight tendency to radicalism in my daughter and my niece.

BOGGS (*from doorway of house.*) Lord de Portment, my Lady.

COUNTESS. Ah! Desire him to come into the garden.
(*Boggs bows and exit.*)
I am really annoyed. (*To Lady I.*) Lord de Portment persists in his attentions to Helena, though he must see that they are distasteful . . .

HELENA. Oh! mamma . . .

COUNTESS. To *me*, at least.

HELENA (*aside to Sappho.*) Again he comes, sweet. So poetic, and so splendidly posed!

SAPPHO. And so fond of you, ah!

LADY I. (*aside to Countess.*) I think I remember de Portment in Lodon. A scrawny man with goggle eyes?

COUNTESS. The same. Lank as a herring.

HELENA (*aside to Sappho.*) And so classic in physique!

SAPPHO. Absolutely attic; ah!

LADY I. (*aside to Countess.*) Yes; very like a yardstick.

COUNTESS. I wish he could remain away. The man is an unmitigated nuisance . . .

(*Enter, from house, de Portment.*)

Ah, my Lord! truly delighted to see you.

(*de P. kisses Countess's hand with great ceremony.*)

Lady Ironsides, Sir Meekly Ironsides, my Lord de Portment.

(*Ceremonious salutes.*)

DE P. To see my Lady Ironsides but once is to remember her forever.

SIR M. (*aside, at back.*) A—amen.

HELENA (*aside to Sappho.*) How gallant!

SAPPHO. Ah, so gallant!

LADY I. We met, I think, at . . .

DE P. Exactly. At the Marchioness of Plumly's fancy ball. *You* appeared as . . .

LADY I. I did. As Brunhild.

COUNTESS (*aside.*) A well chosen character.

Lady I. I remember *your* commanding presence in the dress of—of . . .

de P. Saladin. Really, I should hardly have supposed your memory could retain so trifling an incident. I am profoundly flattered, madam.

Lady I. My Lord, impossible for me to forget, I am sure. (*aside to Countess.*) What a flat he is, to be sure!

Countess. A perfect noodle!

(*Countess and Lady I. go up stage.*)

de P. (*to Helena.*) My dear lady, time's pinions have seemed weighted since last I had this privilege.

Sappho (*aside.*) Ah!

Helena. I' faith, time is but a sorry carrier.

Countess. (*from back.*) Lord de Portment, we are going to look at the rhododendrons on the other side of the garden. Will you not join us?

de P. You will pardon me, my Lady, if I prefer a rosebud to a rhododendron. (*Glancing towards Helena.*)

Countess. A very graceful compliment to Sappho, which I am sure she will appreciate. (*Coming down.*)

Helena (*aside to Countess.*) Oh, mamma! 'twas I whom he meant.

Countess. Of course it was; but I choose to take it otherwise. (*To de P.*) I must really ask you to give your arm to Lady Ironsides, otherwise she would have to be escorted by her husband, and that, you know, would be quite too dreadful.

de P. Oh, quite. Delighted, I'm sure.

(*Offers arm to Lady I.*)

Countess. Sir Meekly, will you take Sappho? You and I, Helena, will lead the way.

Helena (*aside to Countess.*) Cruel mamma.

Countess. Say rather, "Wise mamma." This way, please.

(*Exeunt R., Countess and Helena.*)

Sir M. (*to Sappho.*) It's really . . aw . . I say . . its r' really an aw' awfully f' fine day, is n't it?

Sappho. Quite truly beatific. The sky is sapphire.

Sir M. Y' yes. Very s' sapphire.

(*Exeunt R., Sir Meekly and Sappho.*)

Lady I. (*to de P.*) I want your influence, my Lord, for

the Female Liberation Society. I shall post you a dozen pamphlets on the "Tyranny of Man" to-morrow.

DE P. Aw, charmed I'm sure.

(*Exeunt de Portment and Lady I.*)

LORD TOUCHSTONE. (*heard within house.*) I don't care I tell you; not a fig; do you understand, not a fig?

BOGGS. (*heard within house.*) But, my Lord . . .

TOUCH. (*heard within house.*) Hold your tongue, sir. Daggers and tombstones! Hold your tongue.

(*Enter from house, Lord Touchstone followed by Boggs, trembling.*)

TOUCH. Never tell me the butler was sorry. How dare he serve me a saddle of venison with currant jelly when he knew I wished blackberry jelly, eh? Answer me that, blockhead! Flintlocks and cutlasses! 'Twould irritate a seraph. Don't stand gaping there, but bring me pens and ink.

BOGGS. Y' yes, my Lord. Directly, my Lord.

(*Exit Boggs.*)

TOUCH. I'll write to that rascally tailor about my court coat, and I can keep cooler if I write out here. The villain! to send me home a coat with a plush collar when he knew I wanted silk! Monstrous! Boggs, Boggs.

(*Enter Boggs.*)

BOGGS. Coming, my Lord.

TOUCH. So is Michaelmas! Why didn't you answer when I called, sir?

BOGGS. I did, my Lord, I . . .

TOUCH. Hold your tongue!

BOGGS. Yes, my Lord.

(*Boggs arranges writing materials on table. Lord T. seats himself and takes a dip of ink furiously.*)

TOUCH. (*writing.*) "Idiot! the next time you try to botch a job of tailoring" . . . (*speaks.*) A pest on such pens. Boggs, you're a fool.

BOGGS. Y' yes, my lord.

TOUCH. Quills! Bring me more quills. These are nothing but infernal toothpicks. Zounds! be quick!

(*Exit Boggs, hastily.*)

Touch. (*solus.*) Its perfectly outrageous that, with my naturally calm and benevolent disposition, I should be eternally annoyed and baited by butlers and tailors. I who am so even-tempered—I  . . .

(*Enter Boggs.*)

There, there, there; hurry, will you, stupid? Do you suppose I can wait all day?

Boggs. Yes, my Lord. I mean no, my Lord.

(*Laughter heard off, R.*)

Touch. Shotguns and scimetars! What's that?

Boggs. My Lady, my Lord; and my Lady Il'Ironsides, my Lord; and my Lord de Portment, my Lord, and  . . .

Touch. Hold your tongue, knave. Do you mean to say there's a garden-party here?

Boggs. My Lady's a-showin' some ladies and gentlemen the rhododendremusses, my lord.

Touch. Ugh! Then let me finish my letter and be done with it. (*writing.*)  . . . "Job of tailoring; just sharpen your owl's eyes by jabbing your shears into them a bit, you conceited donkey."  . . .

(*More laughter off, R.*)

(*speaks.*) How boisterous they are! It's positively ungenteel! (*He completes letter.*)

Boggs (*aside.*) I 'opes they'll get back before the H'earl gets another h'attack of choler.

Touch. There, Boggs, take this letter, and see that it's delivered to-day; do you hear?

(*Delivering letter to Boggs.*)

Boggs. Yes, my Lord.

Touch. (*aside.*) Ah, I forgot to sign it. No matter. That dunderhead will know my character. He's seen it before.

(*Laughter nearer, off R.*)

Disgusting hilarity! If there's anything I do admire it's a low voice. These people laugh too loud. It's abominable.

Boggs (*aside.*) There a-comin'. But so is the choler. Its a even race.

Touch. By Hercules! it puts me out of temper. What right, I should like to know.  . .  Oh, they are here.

(*Enter Lady I., R., on the arm of de P.*)

LADY I. Yes, my Lord. One hundred and seventy fish-women bearing banners with the device: "Death to man!" Wasn't it grand?

DE P. Sublime, I'm sure. (*aside.*) Oh heavens! To be talked to death!

LADY I. Lady Touchstone would join our ranks if it were not for that cross-grained old idiot, the Earl . . .

TOUCH. Ahem! Enjoying the garden I see, Lady Iron-sides.

LADY I. (*starting.*) Oh!

TOUCH. Ah, de Portment, good-day.

DE P. Ah, my Lord. (*bowing low.*)

LADY I. Your lordship quite startled me . . .

TOUCH. Yes. I *thought* I startled you. How did you like the rhododendrons?

LADY I. Oh beautiful; but too frail. Flowers, like women, should be strong and vigorous. We want power, *power*, my Lord.

DE P. (*aside.*) Ye powers!

(*Enter, R., Countess and Helena.*)

COUNTESS. I hope Sappho will take good care of Sir Meekly.

HELENA. Poor Sappho. Oh! here's sweet papa.

TOUCH. Yes, here I am, girl. Daggers and brimstone! you've got blue ribbons in your hair again. Now how often have I told you I hate blue ribbons?

Confound it, girl, why will you irritate me in this unbearable manner?

COUNTESS. Dear my Lord, be calm.

TOUCH. Calm, madam, calm? I am calm, perfectly calm, di! di! *diabolically* calm, madam. Razors and rapiers! calm, *calm* indeed! Ha!

LADY I. (*aside.*) The old Turk!

HELENA. Blue sweetly symbolizes the Arcadian firmament, papa.

TOUCH. Arcadian fiddlestick!

(*Sound of hoofs, off L. Boggs looks out of garden gate, C.*)

DE P. A charming seat you have here, my Lord.

2

Touch. Abominably inconvenient, I can assure you. Poor shooting, too, all through the county.

Countess (*aside to Lady I.*) What do you think of de Portment?

Lady I. A polished clam-shell!

Boggs (*from gateway.*) My Lord, Sir Harry Sangfroid is coming h'up the h'avenue at full canter.

Touch. Better that than empty *de*canter, I suppose.

de P. (*clapping his hands elegantly.*) Ha, ha, ha. Very good, my Lord, capital.

(*All laugh.*)

Lady I. (*aside.*) What an elephantine joke!

Touch. *Rather* neat, wasn't it? I was always considered famous at a pun. Ha, ha, ha.

Helena (*aside.*) Puns always did make me shiver; they are *so* commonplace.

Countess. Oh, I'm so glad Sir Harry is coming. He always brightens us up so—like a summer breeze.

Touch. Ugh! Or a tornado.

Sir Harry (*heard without.*) Blanket him well, Jerry; he's steaming like a teakettle. Oh, we've had a splendid run.

Touch. Killing more horses! He's always at it.

Sir H. (*heard without.*) Take care! He is tender in that off hind hoof. Ah, lass; checks as red as ever, eh? Ha, ha, ha. Is your mistress within, Rosebud? Ha, ha, ha, ha.

(*Enter, through gateway, C., Sir Harry, laughing.*)

Countess. Welcome, Sir Harry; you know how charmed we always are to see you.

Sir H. (*kissing Countess's hand.*) Ah, madam, you are too kind. My Lord.

Touch. Glad to see you Sangfroid.

Countess. You know my Lady Ironsides?

Sir H. Oh, intimately. (*Sir H. takes Lady I.'s hand and attempts to raise it to his lips, but she draws it away and bows severely.*) . . . By reputation.

Lady Helena (*kissing her hand*), you grow more beautiful each time I see you.

Touch. (*aside.*) So do cabbages.

Sir H. Ah, de Portment.

(*de P. and Sir H. shake hands.*)

LADY I. (*aside*.)   A horridly forward man!

SIR H.   I miss one flower, Countess, even in so fair a garden.   Is Lady Sappho not here?

COUNTESS.   She is at the lake with Sir Meekly Ironsides. They wanted to see the gold fish.

HELENA.   Yes; such tiny bits of living sunlight, ah!

SIR H.   Then must I keep one pleasure in anticipation.

LADY I. (*to de P.*)   Do you know this butterfly?

DE P.   Very well.   A thoroughly good fellow, your ladyship, really.

TOUCH.   Any news in the city, Sangfroid?

SIR H.   Only that Benson has made up his books on Czarina, and she is now quoted at one to five against the field.

TOUCH.   Egad!   You don't say so.   The Duke of Devonshire will back her; eh?

SIR H.   Oh, for all she's worth.

(*Touchstone offers his snuff-box to Sir Harry, and they both snuff ceremoniously.*)

LADY I. (*to de P.*)   I suppose that is "horse-talk;" is it not?

DE P.   I suppose so.   I am more familiar with mules myself.

LADY I. (*aside*.)   More congenial I should imagine.

COUNTESS.   Sir Harry, do tell me about the de Lacy's musical.   Of course you were there?

SIR H.   Oh, of course.   Well, there was a first movement of a Bach, and a last movement of a Handel, and, as most of the people had gone comfortably to sleep, they crashed out an overture from "Agrippina" to wake them up again.   Ha, ha, ha.

COUNTESS.   Ah, you naughty critic.   Ha, ha, ha.   Did the "Agrippina" have the desired effect?

SIR H.   To be sure.   On the principle of fighting fire with fire.   Your thorough artist will cure an attack of Handel with a dose of Handel, even as a quack will cure madness with the hair of the dog that bit you.

COUNTESS.   Ah, you droll fellow!

HELENA.   So droll!

LADY I. (*to de P.*)   I wonder if he thinks that witty?

DE P.   Original, at least.

Sir H.    But I assure you, my Lady, de Lacy's party was a paragon of life compared with the Baron Gelatin's dinner. Oh heaven!

Touch. (*aside.*)  Now Sangfroid is going to let off one of his incredible stories.

Sir H.    Why, if your Ladyship will credit me, there were forty-two courses, and a different wine with each course.

Lady I. (*aside.*)   A coarse affair!

de P. (*to Lady I.*)   *Fortitude* must have been a prevailing virtue.

Countess.    Forty-two!

Sir H.    Fact, my Lady.  We worked incessantly for four hours, and only got as far as the entrees.

Helena.   I cry you mercy!   What a grievous bore!

Touch.   We pronounce it " boire" in French, girl.

de P.   Oh!

Lady I. (*aside.*)   Another elephantine joke!

Countess.   And was it stupid?

Sir H.   Stupid?   Ye gods!   The Prime Minister spoke for eight hours on . . .

Countess.   Eight hours!

Sir H.   By the watch.

Touch. (*aside.*)   Blood and bodkins!   How superbly he lies!

Sir H.   Eight hours, madam.   And the little pages went around, with the game, to unloose the stocks of the British aristocracy ere they suffocated from excess of loyalty.

Touch. (*aside.*)   Superb!   He has reduced it to a fine art.

Lady I.   A specimen, I suppose, of a *gentlemen's* party. Had there been women present you would have had more brains and less speech making.

Sir H.   Perhaps, madam.

Lady I.   "Perhaps," sir?   I say undoubtedly, sir.   Women cannot much longer be excluded from her rights.

Helena.   To go to dinners?   How material, ah!

Lady I.   The signs of the times are unmistakable, sir; and suffragists have both tongues to speak and ears to hear, let me tell you.

Sir H.   I have no doubt as to the development of both those organs, madam.

Touch. (*aside.*)   Egad!   he hits her hard.

LADY I. (*satirically*.) Sir, you are a wit.

SIR H. Madam, I thank you.

(*A scream is heard off R.*)

TOUCH. Lightning and lunatics! What's the matter now?

COUNTESS. Good heavens! It was Sappho.

(*Sir H. runs up stage. Enter Sappho hurriedly and drops into Sir H.'s arms, R.*)

HELENA. Alack! What bolt of Jove is this?

LADY I. Ladies, be calm! Let us remember that we are women. Leave hysterics to silly men, I beg.

HELENA (*to Sappho.*) Speak, sweet.

SAPPHO. Oh, heavy day! Sir Meekly . . .

LADY I. Eh?

SAPPHO. Sir Meekly—oh!

COUNTESS. Heavens! *What* of Sir Meekly?

SAPPHO. Sir Meekly has—alas!

TOUCH. Pills and perdition, girl! Sir Meekly has what?

SAPPHO. Has fallen into the fish-pond—oh!

(*She falls again into Sir H.'s arms.*)

LADY I. Oh, is *that* all?

DE P. (*aside.*) What an undignified proceeding!

TOUCH. Ye gods! Then let 's get him out.

(*He turns to R. and looks off.*)

COUNTESS. Oh hurry, somebody.

TOUCH. No; it's all right. Boggs has got him out and is fetching him in a wheelbarrow. Egad! he looks a bit uncomfortable. Ha, ha, ha.

HELENA. A wheelbarrow! How disgustingly modern!

SAPPHO. Is he saved? Ah!

LADY I. (*to Sappho.*) Young lady, if you propose to swoon again just take a fresh gentleman. Sir Harry looks tired.

SIR H. On the contrary, I could wish Sir Meekly would remain in the fish-pond for a week.

LADY I. Sir!

SIR H. That is, if he didn't take cold.

(*Enter, R., Boggs pushing Sir M. in a wheelbarrow. He is dripping with water and seems exhausted.*)

DE P. How disagreeably moist!

2*

*(*Boggs wheels barrow to doorsteps.   Sir H. and Touch. assist
Sir M. to rise.*)*

SIR M. (*sitting up in barrow.*)   N' nearly f' food for f' fishes.
Boo 'oh!

LADY I. (*dramatically.*)   Take him in and dry him!

DE PORTMENT.
*

LADY IRONSIDES.                          HELENA.
*                                         *

COUNTESS.                                BOGGS.
*                                         *

SAPPHO.                 TOUCHSTONE.                SIR MEEKLY.
*                          *                          *

SIR HARRY.
*

## ACT SECOND.

SCENE.—*Same as in Act First. Time, the afternoon and evening.*

(*Helena and Sappho enter from L.*)

HELENA. It may be very imprudent in me, sweet, but my Lord de Portment was *so* pressing, and I have promised to give him an interview in the garden so soon as the moon is up. The rest will be well settled at their cards by then, you know.

SAPPHO. Ah, *so* imprudent! Ah, how *I* should like to be imprudent too! Just a little, you know, ah!

HELENA. Stolen grapes always set the teeth on edge, but then . . .

SAPPHO. Moral dyspepsia is such a trifling ill, ah!

HELENA. Methinks Sir Harry,—ah, I caught you blushing, sweet!

SAPPHO. A rose-tint on a cloud. The reflection of your foolish jest upon my frown!

HELENA. What a poetical conceit. Where did you get it?

SAPPHO. From Herrick, dear. I learned it by rote so as to have it ready for an emergency.

HELENA. Now, if Sir Harry should ever make a foolish jest . . .

SAPPHO. Go to! You tease me, Helena.

HELENA. No, on my faith. I overheard him speaking to my own Corinthian-browed de Portment about a little scheme to send you a letter.

SAPPHO. Ha!

HELENA. Nay, 'tis true. A letter asking *you* to meet *him* in the garden. Methinks he loves you, Sappho.

SAPPHO. Ah, can this be true? And yet I hardly know whether I should desire it. Lady Ironsides says that love is *so* enervating.

HELENA. So is summer; and yet methinks eternal winter would scarcely suit our complexion. Has Lady Ironsides said much to you, Sappho?

SAPPHO.  Oh, yes, she has been telling me some wondrous things.  She says it is proven historically that the Creator first made woman out of some particles of pure Celestial brain, and that afterwards, finding an inferior creature necessary, he evolved man from a toad.                              (*a pause.*)

HELENA.  How fortunate that there *were* toads, wasn't it? Else what in the world should have become of us all?

SAPPHO.  I asked Lady Ironsides that, and she replied that we should have lived in a beatific condition of absolute will. She is a great woman on the will, dear!

HELENA.  Superb!  But upon her theory what becomes of that ancient story of the rib and . . . ?

SAPPHO.  An anatomical soap-bubble, invented by man to cheat woman out of the suffrage!  Woman made out of a rib indeed!  Lady Ironsides says you might as well tell her that bon-bons were made out of sausages.

HELENA.  Booh!  what an odious comparison!  Has Lady Ironsides indeed made a convert of you, Sappho?

SAPPHO.  Faith, I hardly know.  I think I shall become a disciple of "the cause," as she terms it.  But I have just embroidered a handkerchief for Sir Harry.  Ivy leaves, sweet. Symbolical, you know.  And it will never do to appear inconsistent.  I am going to be terribly severe with him soon, but I should really like to hear what he has to say first.

HELENA.  In the garden, eh?  But hark!  I hear voices. Let us within.  See how the fiery chariot of the day flings parting glories from his flying wheels.  Let us go to an upper window where our souls may draw an inspiration from the setting sun.

SAPPHO.  Yes . . . and dress for dinner, sweet.
              (*Exeunt to house Helena and Sappho.*)

(*Enter, C., through garden gateway, Sir Harry and Lord de Portment.*)

SIR H.  It's all up, my dear de Portment; I've been for eight and forty hours trying to find out how many times ten will go into five; and I really can't figure it out; 'pon my honor I can't.  Ha, ha, ha.

DE P.  Will you kindly inform me what you intend to convey by the expression, "it's all up"?

SIR H.  A mere figure of speech.  A metaphorical allusion to bankruptcy.  Ha, ha, ha.  I'm absolutely done for . . .

DE P. Horror! "Done for?"

SIR H. Absolutely. Taken in—squeezed—scuttled! Liabilities run into five figures. Assets zero, with a minus mark thrown in. Ha, ha, ha, ha, ha.

DE P. Good heavens! Do you mean that you are . . .?

SIR H. I do. Ruined. That's the word. You see Tamerlane broke within fifty rods of the winning-post—I had four thousand on him. Then Lord Fitz-Maurice got me badly at the Duchess of Lanville's card party, and when I tried to square up with Fitz-Maurice, by doubling my stake on Lady Fleetwood . . .

DE P. Stake on Lady Fleetwood?

SIR H. Yes. She was so splendidly dammed—

DE P. Sir!

SIR H. That I thought I could count on her staying qualities, and . . .

DE P. I beg pardon, Sir Harry. Did I understand you to refer to the spiritual condition of Lady Fleetwood?

SIR H. Spiritual con . . . Ha, ha, ha. Why she's a mare, de Portment.

DE P. Oh!

SIR H. Then, to crown all, I backed the red cards for three thousand guineas at Benson's on Tuesday, and I assure you it was perfectly ludicrous to see every bit of pasteboard turn up black during the rest of the evening. Ha, ha, ha. It was just the funniest thing I ever saw. Ha, ha, ha.

DE P. How can you be so disgustingly light-hearted?

SIR H. Disgustingly light-pursed you ought to say. However, my Lady Touchstone's Madeira will taste none the worse for that, eh, de Portment?

DE P. By the way, speaking of the Touchstones, I think you could be of service to me there, if you would.

SIR H. Delighted, my dear fellow, delighted. Only speak the word. I'll storm a bastion, blow up the grand Turk, or —or—

DE P. Nothing quite so heroic is requisite. I want your influence with the Countess, that is all. I know you are a great favorite with her, and I am sure you can plead my cause.

SIR H. Plead your cause? . . .

DE P.  Yes.  You may perhaps not be aware that I aspire to the hand of the Lady Helena, her daughter.

SIR H. (*aside.*)  The devil!

DE P.  An angel, sir; a very angel . . .

SIR H.  So I was just saying to myself . . .

DE P.  One capable of turning this grovelling sphere of earth into a paradise.

SIR H.  Yes.  They are all capable of doing that—just before marriage.

DE P.  Ah, Sir Harry, you little know how much loveliness . . .

SIR H.  Can be packed in one woman, like gherkins in a pint bottle.  Is that it, de Portment?  But pardon me.

DE P.  In a word, I desire you to speak for me to the Countess.

SIR H.  A kind of double proxy arrangement, eh?

DE P.  A facetious tongue might perhaps term it so.  I assure you, Sir Harry, you will be conferring a favor which I shall not forget.  And, by the way, I have an idea.

SIR H. (*aside.*)  Egad!  I should never have suspected it.

DE P.  You spoke awhile ago of some trifling loans which you wished to negotiate with Isaacs.  Now, if you will permit me to arrange the matter for you . . .

SIR H.  My dear de Portment, I really couldn't think of it.  You are quite too kind.

DE P.  Pray, say no more.  It is only a fair reciprocal arrangement, and if you succeed you will gain for me a boon worth many times all I shall secure for you.

SIR H.  Sir, I shall exhaust my eloquence.

DE P.  Then I regard my suit as won.  Lady Touchstone's preference for you is marked.  I am sure you can win her consent, and as to the Earl I think in this matter he will be guided by my Lady.  So you see how much depends upon you.

SIR H.  Trust me to do my best.  But the effort required will not be great.  I overheard Lady Touchstone tell Lady Ironsides how highly she esteemed you, and how delighted she always was to receive you here. (*aside.*)  Heaven forgive me.

DE P.  You surprise me, and I need not add gratify me beyond expression.  You really think the Countess favors me?

Sir H.  Favors you?  *Dotes* on you, de Portment.  (*aside.*)
I may as well make my devil big enough!

de P.  Well, to be frank, I thought I saw marks of more
than ordinary appreciation, but yet I almost feared to broach
the subject of my attachment for the Lady Helena until . . .

Sir H.  Until you knew your ground.  Quite right, my
dear sir.  I'll prepare the way for you.  But you'll find none
but friends in the camp.  There, for instance, is my Lady
Ironsides.

de P.  Ay, what of *her?*

Sir H.  Captivated with you, my Lord.  Absolutely carried
away.  Told me confidentially that if there was one man in the
world who could lead her to renounce the cause of woman suffrage, that man was Lord de Portment!

De P.  Most extraordinary!

Sir H.  Quite so, indeed.

de P.  But Lady Ironsides struck me as being rather a
severe woman, rather disposed to masculinity . . .

Sir H.  Oh, not at all, not at all.  The gentlest of her sex!
With me she was absolutely shrinking.  (*aside.*)  Deucedly
so, by Jove!

de P.  And she was pleased with me?

Sir H.  Were it not for Sir Meekly, I should call it by a
tenderer name, but . . .

de P.  Ye gods! can it be possible?  Why she spoke to
me about certain pamphlets on the "Tyranny of Man" and
other amiable subjects.

Sir H.  Ah, do you not understand?  Man's tyranny over
the weak and susceptible heart of woman!  Could you not take a
hint?  Ah, some lucky fellows actually have to have a woman's
affections *thrust* upon them!

de P.  Oh, I see it all.  This is, indeed, a revelation!

Sir H.  Quite so, indeed.  Lady Ironsides told me in con-
fidence that she dared not look at you when you smiled.  She
said your smile was a burst of sunlight!

de P.  Strange, strange.

Sir H.  'Tis the brilliancy of your wit, the splendor of your
physique, that have done it all.  I overheard both ladies refer
to you in those particulars.

de P.  And they were enthusiastic?

Sir H. Rapturous! (*aside.*) Egad, I think I'm even with my lady of the suffrage association now.

De P. My dear Sir Harry, let me beg of you to keep this discovery to yourself. I must be discreet, but still I would not absolutely crush a confiding heart. Lady Ironsides, it is true, is not young . . .

Sir H. (*doubtfully.*) N' no.

De P. But then she's not exactly old . . .

Sir H. (*decisively.*) No.

De P. And she would do for practice pending your suit, in my behalf, for the Lady Helena.

Sir H. Ah, cruel Adonis!

De P. No, I would not be cruel; indeed, I would not; but then what can a man do?

Sir H. True; 'tis hard. But let me beg of you not to use that fatal smile.

De P. Well, I'll see about it. And now I'll let you into a secret. Helena is to give me a tête-a-tête this evening.

Sir H. Here?

De P. Here.

Sir H. Better act by proxy.

De P. You?

Sir H. I.

De P. Hum.

Sir H. Be sure of your ground, you know.

De P. Thanks; but there are occasions when principals are better than attorneys.

Sir H. Quite so indeed.

De P. I will meet Helena; but do you press my cause with the Countess. Meanwhile I'll keep myself in practice with old Lady Ironsides—that is—I mean—

Sir H. Ripe womanhood!

De P. Exactly. But it is growing dusk, and I must be back in season for the Earl's whist-table this evening. We shall meet then, I trust?

Sir H. Oh, of course. Remember!

De P. Hist! Be eloquent. *Au revoir.*

Sir H. Farewell, cruel, cruel Adonis!

(*Exit de P. through gateway, C.*)

Sir H. (*solus.*) Now if I haven't put a pretty little bee

into de Portment's bonnet and a pretty little wasp into my Lady Ironsides' reticule, my name is never Sangfroid. Ha, ha, ha. Egad! I'd like to hear him make love to the old girl. Oh, ho, ho, ho.

But I must think of myself. I *must* see Sappho, and I am sure this note will bring her if I can only get it delivered. But how? Ah, what is that? (*Looks off, R.*) By Jove! A winged Mercury in the shape of Boggs; the very messenger I need.

(*Enter R., Boggs pushing barrow.*)

Stop, my good man. I want you to do me a favor.

Boggs. At your worship's service.

Sir H. (*giving him note.*) I wish my Lady Sappho to receive this immediately. And I don't desire that any one should see it delivered. You understand me. (*giving him money.*) This for your trouble. I know you can be silent.

Boggs. Mum as a Yarmouth bloater, Sir 'Arry. And a thousand thanks, Sir 'Arry. (*puts note in his hat.*)

Sir H. Be prompt and you shall not regret it.
(*Exit Sir H. through gateway, C.*)

Boggs. (*solus.*) 'e be a gentleman after my own 'eart, and it would be a 'appy day if Lady Sappho did take likings to 'im. I caught sight of her but now at the side window, and I'll manage to slip her the letter as soon as I put away the barrow; it were jolly wet with Sir Meekly's drainings, but I've dried it out in the sun. He, he, he. Gad, but Sir Meekly are the most unfortunatest gentleman ever I see. But my Lady Meekly! Stars and garters! She be enough for two. Hi, hi.
(*Wheels barrow off, L.*)

(*Enter from house Sir Meekly.*)

Sir M. (*solus.*) I've got over my c' chill and feel c' comparatively c' comfortable; but I wish Lady Ironsides would not set me to spying. H' here she says that she knows there's something in the w' wind, and that I've got to w' watch outside the g' garden wall.

Wonderful w' woman for finding things out. P' powerful creature; powerful c' creature!
(*Exit through gateway, C.*)

3

*(Enter R., Boggs.)*

BOGGS. (*solus.*) Now, then, for the letters. (*takes four letters from his hat.*) Two of 'em came by the post—one for Lady Ironsides and one for my Lord. Then there's the one that Sir 'Arry told me to give to Lady Sappho, and the one that my Lord writ to the tailor. Egad! I ought to have give that to the post; but I forgot, and it 'll have to wait till morning. "Boggs," says the H'earl, "deliver that immejit." That's what they all say. "Yes, my Lord," says I, and that's the end on it till I think of the matter again. Now, by the saints! which is which? Whew! here's a stew! My early education didn't extend to readin' handwritin', more's the pity, and I 'll be blessed if I know t'other from which! 'Ere's one with nothin' on the cover; and 'ere's another that has somethin' on it like a stroke of black lightning. Egad! I 'll have to take chances, and leave the rest to 'eaven.

TOUCHSTONE (*within.*) Boggs, Boggs.

BOGGS. Oh, law! Yes, my Lord.

*(Enter from house, Touchstone.)*

TOUCH. Where the d——, oh, there you are.

BOGGS. Yes, my Lord. A letter for you, my Lord. (*giving letter.*)

TOUCH. Well, give it me, and then be off with you, and tell Edward to have the dogs ready to-morrow at seven. Do you hear!

BOGGS. Yes, my Lord. 'Eaven send it be the right one!
*(Exit, Boggs, L.)*

TOUCH. (*tearing open letter.*) What a fool that man is! Never about when he is wanted. Eh! eh! What's all this? (*reading*) "old brute, the Earl of Touchstone." Sulphur and Lucifer! That's me! me! "Don't see how you can breathe the same air with such a monster." Oh, I'll choke! "Male termagant!" Me, again! Ha! I'll choke! Whose letter *is* this? Mrs. Amadeus Hector, as I live (*referring to cover*), and addressed to Lady Ironsides. I never glanced at the superscription. That stupid owl has given me the wrong letter. Tigers and traitors! Let me—ha! I shall suffocate. "Male termagant." I—a man of my equable temperament! Villainous! That's the way my hospitality is abused. Villainous! Oh ho, I'll deliver this myself. I'll tell my Lady Ironsides, I'll—I'll—boo–oh.

(*Exit to house.*)

(*Enter, L., Boggs.*)

Boggs (*solus.*) A quick job, and a neat one. I slipped Lady Sappho's letter into her 'and at the window, and nobody saw, and that's what Sir 'Arry wanted. Then I met my Lady Ironsides takin' her constitutional on the terrace, and I gave her hers. I 'ope I've made no mistake. A mixin' up might be onpleasant all 'round.

(*Looking off, L.*)

Oh, 'ere she comes. Egad! She looks sort o' h'agitated. I guess I'll go down to the kennels a bit.

(*Exit, R.*)

(*Enter furiously, L., Lady Ironsides, with an open letter in her hand.*)

LADY I. Oh, monstrous! monstrous! To *me !* A woman of my calibre! A love-letter to *me!* The man must be a fool. And signed, too, "Lovingly, Harry!" Oh, oh, I'll—Harry him! Insolent repro . . .

TOUCH. (*within.*) Bait and spring-traps! Let me find her. Let me—oh . . .

(*Enter Touch, from house.*)

Let me just . . . By Jupiter! Ha!

LADY I. Ha! Oh! I've been looking for you, sir . . .

TOUCH. And I for you, madam. Let me tell you . . .

LADY I. Let *me* tell *you*, sir, that . . .

TOUCH. By heaven! I'll not endure it, my Lady, I'll not . . .

LADY I. Endure! Ha! ha, ha. Is your Lordship aware that you are harboring a traitor within your domestic circle?

TOUCH. Yes, by my head! I'm *well* aware of it. Exactly the word—a traitor. I come to deliver you your letter, madam, ha! Your letter, there . . .

LADY I. My letter? Hold! I have my letter, and a pretty letter it is! Insolent rascal to write me such . . .

TOUCH. Audacious gibberish! "Monster," "Male termagant." Ha!

LADY I.    A love letter to me!   Oh, I shall burst!

TOUCH.    By heaven!   I *am* bursting!

. LADY I. (*reading.*)   "Fair charmer: The exquisite handiwork of your fingers has given me hope.   Meet me in the garden before the moon is too high.   I long to hear from your own rosy lips what I cannot but believe is in your heart. Lovingly, Harry."

TOUCH.    Eh!   What, what, what!

LADY I.    Boo—oh!   "Harry!"   That scamp, Sir Harry Sangfroid, of course.   Oh, wait till I see him!

(*It begins to grow dark.*)

TOUCH.    He wrote this to you—to *you*, Lady Ironsides?

LADY I.    Ay, to me!

TOUCH.    He *must* be a fool!

LADY I.    "Rosy lips," indeed!

TOUCH.    Oh, an ass—an idiot!

LADY I.    "Exquisite handiwork!"   A foolscap, I suppose. Oh, but I'll be revenged.   The man's a villain.   Look to your Countess, Lord Touchstone, look to your Countess.

TOUCH.    Demons and darkness!   What do you mean?

LADY I.    Insidious coxcomb!

TOUCH.    And what does this letter mean, madam?   This precious epistle from Mrs. Hector?   I'm "a brute," am I? Ha!

LADY I.    Mrs. Hector? (*she takes letter.*)   Permit me to compliment your Lordship on your skill in breaking seals.

TOUCH.    An accident, an accident.   But look at the contents.   . . .   Perdition! look at the contents.

LADY I.    At my leisure, sir.   Look to your Countess. Traitors are traitors, sir.

TOUCH.    Zounds!   So I've discovered, madam.   "A brute!" Pish!   "A monster!"

(*It grows dark.*)

LADY I.    "Fair charmer!"   "Rosy lips!"   Ha! the wretch!

TOUCH.    Aha!   Knives and napkins!   "Brute!"   Bah!

(*Touch. rushes out through gateway, C.*)

LADY I.    "Lovingly, Harry!"   Villain!   Ha!

(*Lady I. rushes off, R.*)

SIR MEEKLY (*peering over garden wall.*)   I w' wonder w' what it's all about.

(*Enter, R., Boggs. Sir M.'s head disappears behind wall.*)

Boggs (*reflectively.*) · I think somethin's wrong. Lady H'ironsides have got her war paint on, as sure as eggs is eggs!
(*Moonlight effect.*)

She near upset me! Jemima! what a speed she has on, to be sure. Rushed past me like a pack at full cry, and never saw me.

I have a undescribable forebodin' that I've mixed them letters up. Egad! I pity the one who gets the tailor's; and I pity myself when the H'earl finds out about it. Oh, Boggs, Boggs, why wasn't you educated to read writin'?
(*Exit, R.*)

(*Enter, L. U. E., Sir Harry and Sappho.*)

Sappho. Is it not beautiful? Each humblest shrub a point of tender light. Each drop of dew a pearl that holds the moon.

Sir H. Yet no pearl's light so mimics the soft moon as do the eyes of one who calls them fair.

Sappho. What one, Sir Harry?

Sir H. Oh, t'were hard to guess. Yet, if you'll keep a secret, I'll be frank, and say I name her *Sappho*.

Sappho. Oh, you confuse me. But since you *will* praise, *do* I look better with a bang or no?

Sir H. With anything that leaves you Sappho still.

Sappho (*aside.*) How glad I am I embroidered him that handkerchief.

Sir H. My note was sent so late, I almost feared me that you would not come.

Sappho. Indeed it *was* late; and, to speak truth, I have not yet had time to read the note. You came upon its very heels, and so I thrust it in my dress, unopened.

Sir H. Ah? Well, it was but a faint expression of my truest thought, and referred to your fair handiwork—the lovely handkerchief with ivy leaves.

Sappho. A trifle. Shall you dance to-night?

Sir H. Perhaps. I hope your fair cousin Helena will not be so cruel as to deny de Portment a quadrille.

Sappho. I suppose not. She is in the drawing-room, now, —busily crocheting a bouquet holder, ah.

3*

SIR H.  Within the drawing-room—and on so lovely a night?

SAPPHO.  Oh yes.  Helena never exposes herself to the night air.

SIR H.  Indeed.

*(Exeunt R. U. E.)*

*(Sir Meekly's head appears over garden wall.  Enter, R. 1 E., de Portment and Helena.  Sir Meekly's head suddenly disappears.)*

DE P.  And do you give all your confidences to Lady Sappho?

HELENA.  Not *quite* all.  Dear Sappho's health is so fragile that she can't sympathize with all my recreations, you know. She never can go even near the window after dark.  Poor Sappho!

DE P.  It must indeed be a deprivation.

HELENA.  Yes, she never knew how beautiful is moonlight under the open sky.  She is playing at chess at this moment with papa.

DE P.  Quite a check to happiness.

HELENA.  Yes, or to your opponent's king.  Do you read poetry, my Lord?

DE P.  I revel in it, sweet lady.  Poetry to me is the final expression of the heart's ambition . . .

HELENA.  Ah!

DE P.  The sweetest chord in the harmony of the spheres  . .

HELENA.  Oh–h!

DE P.  The very essence of love's rarest flower.

HELENA.  Ah–h–h!

*(Exeunt R. U. E.)*

SIR M. *(peering over wall.)*   P' paradise boiled d' down!
*(Suddenly ducks his head.)*

*(Enter L. U. E., Sir Harry and Sappho.)*

SIR H. So soon?  Ah, Sappho, you are like those Eastern queens who reign but to be cruel.  Why must you go so soon?

SAPPHO.  I shall be missed; and then, you know, dear Helena must be *so* lonely.

SIR H.  True.  But I am hardly unselfish enough to think of her just now.

SAPPHO. Adieu.

SIR H. Say rather *au revoir*. In half an hour I shall see you in the drawing-room.

SAPPHO. Oh, 'twill be half a week. My pent up heart dare trust itself no more; but time drags like a laggard till you come. Love is so peremptory.

SIR H. And so passing fair.

SAPPHO. And all the heart so sweetly sanguine. Ah!— Is my hair mussed?

SIR H. Not a bit.

SAPPHO. Farewell. (*He kisses her on the forehead.*)

SIR M. (*peering over wall.*) Oh–h–h!
(*Ducks his head suddenly.*)
(*Exit Sappho to house.*)

(*Enter, R. U. E., de Portment and Helena. They cross the stage at back. At centre de P. bends over Helena, and Sir Harry covers his face with his hat and skips behind bushes at L. Then exeunt de P. and Helena at L. U. E*)

(*Enter from house Countess, with opera cloak over her arm.*)

COUNTESS (*calling.*) Helena, Helena. Where can she have gone? It's growing chill, and I must seek her. Helena!
(*Exit Countess, R. U. E.*)

SIR H. (*coming out from bushes.*) Egad! This is my opportunity to do de Portment a double service. I'll give him a chance for five more words with Helena, and follow the Countess to plead his cause for him according to promise. Fate favors us to a charm.
(*Exit Sir H., R. U. E.*)

(*Enter L. U. E., de Portment and Helena.*)

HELENA. Indeed, my Lord, 'tis growing late, and I thought I heard mamma calling.

DE P. Only the screeching of an early owl, I—I mean the trill of an early nightingale. Do not go, sweet Helena.

HELENA. Indeed I must. Dear Sappho must be so tired of that game of chess. Poor Sappho, she little knows how sweet a thing is love, ah–h!

DE P. Little indeed.
(*de P. kneels on one knee at steps, and kisses her hand.*)

HELENA.   Alas! So brief! Adieu.

DE P.   Adieu.

(*Exit Helena to house.*)

SIR M. (*over wall.*)   Oh–h–h!

(*Ducks his head.*)

(*Enter, R. U. E., Sir Harry and Countess.   He is in the act of putting cloak around her shoulders.   de Portment covers his face with his hat, and skips behind bushes at L.*)

SIR H.   My dear Countess, you know that I am a loyal friend, and I would fain speak for de Portment as for myself. Will you not sit here for a moment?

COUNTESS.   For a moment.   The night is so charming.

SIR H.   Pray let me draw your cloak closer.   'Tis somewhat chilly.   So.

DE P. (*from bushes, aside.*)   By Jove!   Splendid!   What a tactician he is!   He pleads for me like a hero.   I'll retire. I am sure she'll yield before his eloquence.

(*Exit L.*)

COUNTESS.   And do you think my Lord de Portment really all he pretends to be?

SIR H.   So far as position is concerned—yes.   As for his affection  .  .  .

COUNTESS.   Oh, that's a matter of no account whatever. Helena will do very nicely without affection; but to marry beneath her would be absolute ruin, you know.

SIR HARRY.   Quite so, indeed.   But de Portment stands well; hob-nobs at the best clubs, and is received by the Devonshires.

COUNTESS.   Ahem!   That's a point in his favor; but he goes to the Boodles.

SIR HARRY.   Only incidentally, I assure you.   He avoided dancing with Clarissa Boodles on her fête-day, and only led Lady Boodles through one figure of the minuet. (*Aside.*)   A lie, but for friendship's sake.

COUNTESS.   I am glad he had so much discretion.   Does he pay his wagers well?

SIR H.   Like a man.

COUNTESS.   And is popular at the races?

SIR H.   Quite so, indeed.

COUNTESS (*reflectively.*) Hum.

SIR M. (*aside, peering over wall.*) Oh, h' heaven! He's g 'got the C' Countess now! (*disappears.*)

SIR M. All I ask is that you will give de Portment a chance to present his credentials, and I ask it for *my* sake.

COUNTESS (*softening.*) Ah!

SIR H. The attitude of a suppliant would perhaps move you (*falling on one knee.*) You see how humility may have its power, eh, my Lady? (*he takes her hand.*)

(*Sir M. appears in gateway endeavoring to hear what is said.*)

COUNTESS. Ah, you hypocrite! You well know how ready I always am to listen to your prayers.

SIR M. (*aside.*) The deuce!

SIR H. And I am sure I shall not now sue in vain.

SIR M. (*aside.*) Oh, by G' George! I can't stand this. I'll run and t' tell Lord T' Touchstone.

(*Exit through gateway.*)

COUNTESS. Well, perhaps not. Mind, I only say *perhaps.* I tell you frankly that I don't like Lord de Portment, but if you think he'll be very discreet . . .

SIR H. Oh, my life on it!

COUNTESS. And will not call upon Helena oftener than once a fortnight . . .

SIR H. I promise it.

COUNTESS. And will only touch her hand in salutation . . .

SIR H. He would never dream of more.

COUNTESS. And will drop the Boodles . .

SIR H. He will.

COUNTESS. And cultivate the Devonshires . . .

SIR H. He shall.

COUNTESS. Why then . . we'll think about it.

SIR H. Ah, I knew you would; you are so kind. (*rises.*)

COUNTESS. By the way, Sir Harry, I hear that Tamerlane lost the race the other day.

SIR H. (*slowly.*) Y' yes.

COUNTESS. I hope you had nothing staked on him?

SIR H. Not a penny! But I won heavily on Lady Fleetwood.

COUNTESS. Excellent! You are *so* lucky!

SIR H.   Oh, am I not?   Ha, ha, ha.   But the funniest thing
was to see me squeeze Fitz Maurice at the Duchess of Lanville's the other night.

COUNTESS.   Oh, I'm so glad; I hate Fitz Maurice.   Ha,
ha, ha.

SIR H.   Took him fairly for four thousand!   The finest run
of aces and kings your Ladyship ever beheld!   Ha, ha, ha.

COUNTESS.   Capital, capital!   But I am forgetting time.
I must go in to my guests.

SIR H.   Forgive me for keeping you so long.   But ere you
go, give me your final promise for de Portment.

*(On one knee, taking her hand.)*

*(Enter through gateway, C., Sir Meekly and Lord Touchstone.)*

SIR H.   You know this is a question of the heart.

TOUCH.   Fiends and . . . !

*(Sir M. places his hand over Touchstone's mouth and motions
him to restrain himself.)*

SIR H.   And questions of the heart demand the gentlest
consideration.

COUNTESS.   Well, I will not deny so eloquent a plea, and
. . .

SIR H.   Thanks.   Though I feel that thanks are but a poor
return.

*(Touch. shakes his fist at Sir Harry.   Exeunt Touch. and Sir
M. through gateway.)*

SIR H.   Must you go in?

COUNTESS.   Indeed I must.   Will you not join our whist
to-night?

SIR H.   Right soon.

*(Sir H. hands Countess up steps to house.   Exit Countess.)*

*(Enter, L. U. E., de Portment.)*

DE P.   Ah, my dear Sir Harry, a thousand thanks.   I heard
the beginning of your interview with her Ladyship, and there-
fore fear nothing for the end.

SIR H.   I am glad to say your suit is won.   The Countess
gives her consent to your paying your addresses to the Lady
Helena.

De P. Without restrictions?

Sir H. Well, she shouldn't like you to call oftener than twice a day—just for the present. It will take a little time to gain the Earl's consent, you know . . .

De P. Oh, I'm not afraid of that. The Earl is, after all, an easy-going man—at times really gentle, and . . .

(*Enter through gateway, Sir M. and Touchstone.*)

Touch. (*ferociously.*) Furies and blue fire! Here you are, sir, at last. You infernal . . . you outrageous . . .

Sir H. Good heavens! my Lord, what is the meaning of this?

Touch. You rascally traitor, you . . .

Sir H. Sir! do you dare apply this language to me?

Touch. Yes, sir, I do. Fiends and rockets! I do, sir. I demand instant satisfaction, Sir Harry Sangfroid; instant, sir.

Sir H. Lord Touchstone, I have not the remotest idea what the matter is; but neither do I care to know. Your insults are sufficient. I refer you to my friend, Lord de Portment, who will arrange everything.

De P. Honored, I am sure. I have a case of duelling-pistols in the box of my coach . . .

Touch. Torches and turnbuckles! Fetch them, sir, fetch them.

(*Exit, L., de Portment.*)

Sir Meekly will act as my second.

Sir M. (*aside.*) Oh, l' law . . . I . . . I . . .

Touch. I have already despatched a messenger for a surgeon.

Sir M. (*aside.*) A 's surgeon! Oh! m' mercy on us.

Touch. What distance do you desire, Sir Harry?

Sir H. Nine paces, my Lord.

Touch. Good, sir, good; seven, if you like.

Sir M. (*aside.*) Kind h' heaven! What a m' murderous pair!

Sir H. Anything to oblige your Lordship. Five, if you choose. It's quite immaterial.

Sir M. (*aside.*) Boo-oh! I wish I had s' said nothing. My blood c' curdles!

(*Enter, L. U. E., de P. with case of pistols.*)

DE P. Everything is in order, gentlemen. Moon bright; no clouds; and we can place you so that there will be no shadow to interfere with a careful aim by both parties. There's a fine bit of ground behind the ten-pin alley, where we can have a nice quiet time.

SIR M. (*aside.*) "Quiet." "Nice." I wish I was home.

DE P. Sir Meekly acts for you, I presume, my Lord?

TOUCH. Yes, sir. And be good enough to be quick. Shot and sabres! Quick!

(*de P. opens case and presents to Sir M.*)

SIR M. (*drawing back.*) W' what do you want of *me*? (*aside.*) I wish Lady Ironsides was here.

DE P. Your choice, Sir Meekly; unless you desire to superintend a reloading.

SIR M. Oh, n' not at all, n' not at all.

DE P. (*bowing.*) I pledge you my honor that both contain double charges.

SIR M. (*aside.*) M' merciful powers!

DE P. Your choice, sir.

(*Sir M. timidly takes one of the pistols, and holds it at a distance; de P. bows and presents the other pistol to Sir Harry.*)

TOUCH. (*impatiently.*) Hurry, Sir Meekly; hand over the other iron, will you?

SIR M. Y' yes, my Lord. (*He hands Touch. pistol.*)

DE P. All ready, gentlemen.

(*Sir Harry and Touch. pass up, and stand bowing ceremoniously at gateway. Finally Touch. passes through; then Sir H. Sir M. and de P. do precisely the same, till finally de P. passes through.*)

SIR M. (*solus*). Oh, h' horror! This will make c' cold m' meat of some of us!

(*Exit through gateway.*)

(*Enter, R. U. E., Boggs.*)

BOGGS (*solus.*) Egad! Now I'm *sure* there's somethin' wrong (*looking out.*) There they go, the whole four. Four together always means whist, or a duel; and I'll swear they

wouldn't play whist by moonlight. Yes, they are making for
the ten-pin alley. Alack! I'd better go down to pick up the
pieces.

(*Exit through gateway.*)

(*Enter hastily from house, Sappho, with an open letter in her
hand.*)

SAPPHO (*sola.*) Oh, oh! Insulted! Trampled upon!
The monster! *This* was his letter; this the letter which I
have been carrying around, thinking it was full of tenderness.
This the epistle I have pressed to my heart, even as Cleopatra
did the asp. He said I was like an Eastern queen. Vampire!
And he told me the letter referred to my handiwork. Oh, oh,
hypocrite! I could read the words even if there were no moon
(*referring to letter.*) "Idiot! The next time you try to botch
a job of tailoring"—Oh, oh, he calls an embroidered handkerchief a job of tailoring! "Sharpen your owl's eyes by jabbing your shears into them." Oh, oh. "Conceited donkey!"
Oh, oh, oh. Fiend! fiend! Why is there not a thunderbolt?
Ha! (*Double report of pistol off left.*)

(*Enter hurriedly from house Countess, Helena, and Lady I.*)

HELENA. Gramercy! What is this?
COUNTESS. What's the matter? Where is Boggs?
HELENA (*running to Sappho.*) What is it, sweet?
SAPPHO. "Conceited donkey!" Oh!
HELENA. Great Juno! What?
LADY I. Ladies, be calm. Emotion is unseemly in *our*
sex.

(*Enter at gateway Boggs.*)

COUNTESS. Speak, Boggs. What has happened?
BOGGS. The gentlemen have just settled a difference, your
Ladyship.
COUNTESS. Good heavens! A duel?
BOGGS. The same, my lady. My Lord and Sir 'Arry, my
Lady.
HELENA (*to Sappho.*) How sweetly mediæval, sweet.
SAPPHO. Sir Harry! Oh, mercy! Is he hurt?
BOGGS. Neither of the principals has got so much as a
scratch.

4

Sappho (*to Helena.*) That is quite modern, dear.

Helena. But the seconds? My Lord de Portment. Oh, what of *him?*

Countess. Boggs, be quicker. Don't keep us in this terrible suspense, man.

Boggs. Well, my Lord fired at the County of Suffolk—and missed it. And Sir 'Arry he fired in the air—and hit Sir Meekly.

Countess. Sir Meekly!

Lady I. (*coolly.*) In the head?

Boggs. No; in the foot, my Lady.

Countess. Oh, this is dreadful!

Sappho. How it will interfere with the quadrilles!

Helena. Shockingly!

Boggs. Then my Lord, becomin' excited, h'accidentally discharged his weapon a second time, and carried off the tip of his right ear.

Countess. What! His own?

Boggs. No, my Lady, Sir Meekly's.

Countess. Oh!

Lady I. (*aside.*) Both ears would bear a shortening.

Countess. Oh, but he must be looked to at once! Where are the gentlemen?

(*Enter, through gateway, de P. Exit Boggs.*)

de P. Pray do not be agitated, ladies! I must apologize for this slight annoyance which honor has rendered necessary. But I assure you the affair was one of the most *recherché* at which I have ever had the pleasure to assist. Lord Touchstone's foresight had provided a surgeon, and we have made Sir Meekly as comfortable as possible.

Countess. But how came he to be hit?

de P. In point of fact, my Lady, Sir Harry, having no personal quarrel with my Lord Touchstone, fired in the air; and as Sir Meekly had climbed a tree . . .

Helena. A tree!

Sappho (*aside.*) Arbor vitæ.

de P. He received the charge in his foot.

Countess. Oh, dear me!

Lady I. Did it shiver the limb?

de P. Of the tree, madam?

LADY I.  Of Sir Meekly, sir.

DE P.  Not at all; I regret the wound in his ear, as that resulted from excitement—an element always *de trop* in duels. But for the rest, everything was perfect.  My Lady, I salute you.

(*Kissing Helena's hand.*)

HELENA.  Ah!

(*Sappho looks at them and sighs languishingly.*)

(*Enter, through gateway, Touchstone and Sir Harry, arm in arm, chatting and laughing.  Enter, behind them, Sir Meekly, on a crutch and cane, left foot bandaged and held up by a strap.  Large bandage over right ear and across his temples.  He is partially supported by Boggs.*)

LADY I. (*aside.*)  There is the villain who dared to write me the love letter.  Oh, he must be punished!

TOUCH.  It's all right, ladies.  Roses and sunflowers! all right.  I made an absurd mistake.  Explanations have followed, and Sir Harry and I are the best of friends.

LADY I.  And Sir Harry and *I* are the worst of enemies.

SIR H.  I?  ⎫
COUNTESS.  What? ⎬
HELENA.  Oh!  ⎭

LADY I.  He has dared to address me in terms of passionate love.

(*Sappho swoons into chair.*)

LADY I. (*pointing to Sir Harry.*)  Sir Meekly, you must have that man out, at once.

SIR M.  M' my love, I f' feel as if s' somebody had had m' me out!

BOGGS.

\*

SIR MEEKLY.

\*

| DE PORTMENT. | | TOUCHSTONE. |
|:---|:---:|---:|
| \* | SAPPHO. | \* |
| HELENA. | \* | SIR HARRY. |
| \* | | \* |
| LADY I. | | COUNTESS. |
| \* | | \* |

## ACT THIRD.

SCENE.—*Drawing-room in the country residence of the Earl of Touchstone. At right, door opening to garden. Fireplace and mantel, with mirror, centre of flat. Easy chairs, right, front. Small table left. Card-tables at left, back.—Time, the evening.*

(*Touchstone and Countess discovered playing at chess, L.*)

TOUCH. Nothing of the sort, I tell you. The letter referred to me. And not only that, but here she is putting all kinds of rubbish into the girls' heads about the rights and dignity of woman. Egad! she'll have us all by the ears soon.

COUNTESS (*making a move on chess-board.*) It can do no harm. The girls have common sense below the surface.

TOUCH. Ugh! A long way below it. I overheard Lady Ironsides instructing Helena and Sappho in the way they should act towards their admirers,—and, by zounds! I believe they are both converted to her way of thinking. They are going to begin showing their superiority this very night. Ho, ho, ho, what a world of imbeciles this is! Ho, ho, ho!
(*Making a move on chess-board.*)

COUNTESS. Lady Ironsides seemed terribly indignant at Sir Harry.

TOUCH. Oh, ha, ha, ha; fugues and fiddlesticks! 'twas as good as a play. Ho, ho, ho.

COUNTESS. And how absurd, to be sure. I give you check.
(*Making a move.*)

TOUCH. Eh! Check! How's that? Hang it! I thought my king was covered. If there is anything which irritates me it is to be suddenly checked. Zounds! It's villainous, I say, villainous!

COUNTESS. Then I'll change my move . . .

TOUCH. Nothing of the sort. I am not a child, madam; you seem to intimate that I have to be humored. Now, by my life! . . .

COUNTESS. Oh, not in the least . . .

Touch. Whereas you must know that I am a singularly amiable person. Surely you can see that nothing but extreme provocation ever irritates me. I make it a point to govern myself absolutely. Absolutely, madam. But I don't like contradiction, you know. And, by Saturn's rings! madam, I'll not have it. I—I . . .

Countess. My Lord, I shouldn't think of contradicting you . . .

Touch. I don't see why Sappho didn't play with me any how. She was to have done so, but got a sick headache suddenly, and had to go to her room. Very mysterious!

(*Making a move.*)

Countess. Poor girl! She is so frail. And she was so shaken up by that unfortunate affair . . .

Touch. A little mistake; that was all. Ha, ha, ha! It *was* ridiculous. But you must admit that things looked bad. And Sangfroid is such a devil of a fellow. To think of his making love to old Ironsides! Oh, Goody-two-shoes! Oh, ho! Odds bodkins! Oh, ho! Hello!

(*Enter dejectedly from garden, Sappho.*)

Countess. My dear girl; how very imprudent of you to be in the garden so late. I thought you were within.

Sappho. No; I wanted to weep at the yellow moon awhile.

Touch. Cheerful occupation! Did the moon seem to enjoy it?

Sappho. The moon herself is but a tear—a Jovian tear.

Touch. Egad! Jove must get rid of a good deal of celestial misery if he sheds it in globules like that; ha, ha.

Sappho. Oh dear! (*Sighs.*)

Countess. Really, Sappho, there appears to be something unusual the matter with you. How is your head, dear?

Sappho. Worse—ah.

Countess (*making a move on chess-board.*) I queen my pawn, please.

Touch. Now, by the Pope's toe! How did you do that? That's what comes of this infernal weeping of moons! Pikes and powder! I'll not finish such a game. The idea of trying to play chess with two women buzzing about yellow moons! By heaven! it's preposterous, it's . . .

Countess. Oh, my Lord . . .

4*

Touch. No, madam, no. I'll not finish such a game, I tell you. It's a trap—a trap to mate me! Ha! I'll not endure it. Bah!

(*Exit L.*)

Countess. Alas! I wish *you* could have played with him, Sappho . . .

Sappho. Thanks very much. I hate stale mates.

Countess. And prefer knights to pawns, I suspect. I must go calm your uncle. He'll be very dyspeptic if he doesn't get quieted.

(*Exit L.*)

Sappho. Poor aunt! What a hard time she has! I wonder if Lord Touchstone was ever statuesque, and told pretty lies by moonlight—ah.

(*Takes letter from pocket and refers to it.*)
" Job of tailoring !" Oh, oh.

(*Enter from garden, Sir Harry.*)

Sir H. (*aside.*) Alone! An unexpected happiness—(*aloud*) Sappho.

Sappho (*turning.*) Ha! monster!

Sir H. Eh!

Sappho. Is it possible you have the audacity to show yourself—to speak to me?

Sir H. Sappho!

Sappho. Again? How dare you approach me, sir?—Oh, oh; you " referred to my handiwork" in your note, did you? You gave me your opinion, did you? Oh, oh, oh (*hysterically.*)

Sir H. Good heavens! Sappho . . .

Sappho (*backing Sir H. into a corner.*) I scorn you,—I scorn your opinion,—I scorn your letter,—I scorn everything about you, sir. Thus do I fling your words from me, sir (*throwing letter on floor.*) Oh, to be deceived! Oh, traitor! traitor! Oh!

(*Rushes out R.*)

Sir H (*solus.*) Is this a tornado or an earthquake? What can it mean? By Jove, my head swims. My . . .

(*Takes up letter from floor.*)

*(Enter L., Lady Ironsides.)*

LADY I. Oh, here you are, insinuating hypocrite! So you thought you could make love to *me*, did you?

SIR H. Heaven forfend, madam!

LADY I. You dared to suppose that I would take a moonlight walk with you, did you? Ha! Do I look like a woman to take moonlight walks, sir? Eh, sir?

SIR H. Not a particle, on my honor . . .

LADY I. *(backing Sir H. into a corner.)* Audacious traitor! Thus do I scorn you and your advances *(throwing letter on the floor.)* Do not think you shall escape punishment. Oh, no, no. Never think it! Never think it. Bah! Pish! Boo–oh!

*(Rushes out R.)*

SIR H. *(after a pause.)* On the whole, I think it may be called an earthquake! A hailstorm of rejected letters. In the name of the Furies, what does it all mean?

*(Takes up second letter.)*

Good gracious! Why, this is my note to Sappho! Oh, ho, ho! No wonder the old lady thinks me audacious. Oh! ha, ha, ha! But what, then, did Sappho receive?

*(Refers to first letter.)*

Eh, what's this?

*(Enter L., Touch. followed by Boggs.)*

TOUCH. Place the whist tables in the library.

BOGGS. Yes, my Lord.

TOUCH. Ah, Sangfroid!

SIR H. My Lord, this letter appears to be in your character. Can you explain it? It begins rather forcibly— *(Reads.)* "Idiot: The next time you try to botch a job of tailoring" . . .

*(Boggs looks horrified and runs out L.)*

TOUCH. Why, bludgeons and broomsticks! that's my letter to that rascally tailor. Boggs, how's this . . . Eh? He's gone. Oh, that lunkhead has made another mistake about the letters! I'll teach him. Boggs, Boggs, you rascal! Oh, I'll warm you up!

*(Exit L.)*

LADY I. *(heard off R.)* Yes, and I haven't done with him yet. I've something else to say to him, and I'll say it now.

SIR H. Oh, heaven! I'll cool myself off.

*(Runs out to garden.)*

*(Enter, R. I. E., Lady Ironsides.)*

LADY I. Not here? He got away very quickly. A guilty conscience always keeps a man moving. Oh, when women get into Parliament, I hope they'll pass an Act to put such fellows permanently in the stocks, and feed them by the year out of the parish funds! Ha!

*(Enter, L. C. E., de Portment with an exaggerated smile on his face, and his head affectedly bent to one side. He comes slowly down, gazing upon Lady Ironsides.)*

LADY I. *(aside.)* What masquerading trick is this? . . . The creature is surely lunatic! . . .

*(de P. approaches, smiling yet more.)*

I knew de Portment was a fool, but I never supposed him capable of such a hideous grimace. *(aloud.)* Well, sir?

DE P. Benign enchantress! *(sighs.)*

LADY I. Eh! *(aside.)* Heavens! I wonder if he has colic.

*(de P. stands smiling at her.)*

What a contortion! A *man* would faint at such a sight. *(aloud.)* What's the matter, sir?

DE P. Fair disturber of my heart's peace!

LADY I. Sir! I?

DE P.. You, fair one, you.

LADY I. Oh, this is simply abominable . . . Sir . . . ,

DE P. Since I beheld your face I know no rest.

LADY I. Lord de Portment, what is the meaning of this?

DE P. Love has robbed me of rest. My peace of mind has vanished. Ah . . .

LADY I. Well, young man, I'll give you a piece of *my* mind in short order. I'd have you to understand . . .

DE P. Nay, nay; I know how you strive to cover womanly coyness with an assumed asperity. But the truth is potent. Harsh words will not long remain upon those rosebud lips.

(*Lady I. screams.*)

Dear one, not so loud; it will alarm the house, and terminate this blissful interview.

LADY I. That is precisely what I intend, insolent intruder! How dare you?

DE P. Love dares all things. I do but come to tell you that I know all, and that I reciprocate your feelings; that I . . .

LADY I. (*aside.*) They 're *all* making love to me; to *me!* What madness is this?

DE P. That I . . . that I . . . in fact that I live but in the light of your . . . your . . . *opal* eyes. (*smiles afresh.*)

LADY I. Hold! hold! No more, or, by my life! I shall forget you are the weaker vessel, and strike you down! Oh, be well assured you shall pay dearly for your insolence. Oh! you wretched, . . . conceited . . . unbearable . . . *coxcomb,* you. To me! To *me!* . . . Boo-oh!

(*Rushes out, R.*)

DE P. (*solus.*) She covers her affection admirably. Poor thing! What it must cost her! She speaks exceedingly *forcibly,* I must confess. But my appearance has evidently made a deep impression.

(*Going up to mirror.*)

And, in fact, I think my figure *is* calculated to make an inroad on feminine susceptibilities. Ah, how wonderful a thing is a thoroughly graceful carriage! Poor ladies! They flicker about, like moths about a candle, but are sure to fly into the flame at last. Ah me! (*Kissing his hand to his reflection.*) Ta, ta. So, so.

(*Enter, L. U. E., Boggs, rubbing his head; as de P. is backing from mirror, he and Boggs collide.*)

BOGGS. Beg pardon. I didn't h'observe your Lordship was h'exercisin'. Your Lordship bade me h'inform you when Lady Helena came down. She's in the conservatory now, my Lord.

DE P. Ah! very good. Is your master there, as well?

BOGGS. Oh no, my Lord. He is *elsewheres.* (*aside.*) I've

reason to know. He's been h'admonishin' me about the letters in a werry powerful manner. (*aloud.*) Lady Helena is alone, my Lord.

(*Exit to garden.*)

DE P. (*solus.*) I go to complete another conquest ; to make my first official court to the fair Helena. How busy these little matters of the heart keep a man ! Ah !

(*Exit L. U. E.*)

(*Enter, from garden, Sir Harry and Boggs.*)

BOGGS. . Lor! Sir 'Arry, but it will be a sort of a revolution, as the 'istorians say. My h'eyes !

SIR H. Never mind. Do as I say. Deliver the messages exactly as I told you, and everything will come out right. Where is Sir Meekly now ?

BOGGS. I've no right to know anythink h'official like, but I do 'appen to know individooally, Sir 'Arry, that he is in the neighborhood of the conservatory. He, he, he !

SIR H. (*aside.*) That elderly dragon has got him on duty again.

BOGGS. Sir Meekly be tolerably well spavined by his mishaps, but he gets about pretty spruce, notwithstandin'.

TOUCH. (*heard off L.*) Pugs and poodles ! Such mistakes irritate me ; they irritate me !

BOGGS. Oh, if you don't want me partickler, Sir 'Arry, I've somethin' immejit to attend to.

SIR H. Ha, ha. Very well ; you had better go.

(*Exit R., Boggs.*)

Poor fellow. I fear Lord Touchstone doesn't keep him on a bed of roses.

(*Enter L., Touchstone.*)

Ah, my Lord ! I hope you won't inconvenience yourself further about the letters. The matter is really of no consequence.

TOUCH. But to think of the fellow's carelessness ! It sets me wild.

SIR H. We should rather pity his disadvantages than blame his carelessness. I trust, as a favor to me, that your Lordship will not be severe.

Touch. Oh, well—of course, if you put it in that light.

Sir H. Thanks. It really seems as if *nothing* should annoy one in this lovely retreat—this quiet spot.

(*A crash of glass, etc., heard off L.*)

Touch. Cats and canister! Quiet! Deucedly quiet! What has happened now?

(*Enter, L. U. E., de Portment.*)

de P. Nothing, my Lord; absolutely nothing. I was endeavoring to say a few words to the Lady Helena in the conservatory, when Sir Meekly Ironsides broke through the roof.

Touch. Ye gods!

de P. For some unknown reason he attempted to climb out, and as his cane slipped, he crashed through the sash, and fell at our feet amid a shower of splintered glass and wood . . .

Touch. Is he hurt?

de P. Considerably scratched about the face. They'll fix him up with court-plaster. It was very discomposing to our conversation—really.

Sir H. And somewhat startling to Lady Helena, eh?

de P. Y' yes. But the fact is, she hardly seemed in a mood to be startled. I think . . . that is, I infer . . . that Lady Ironsides has been talking to her.

Sir H. And I am sure of it.

Touch. Egad! I told you so, I told you so. Oh, she'll have us all by the ears!

de P. Lady Helena was very . . . *distrait*. In point of fact, she desired me to confine my conversation to geology . . .

Sir H. Oh, ha, ha, ha, ha, ha, ha!

Touch. Geol . . . Oh, ho, ho, ho!

de P. Whereas, as your Lordship must, of course, be aware, I had intended paying my most ardent addresses, and . . .

Touch. Geology! Oh, cubes and cobblestones! Geology! Oh, ho, ho!

de P. And the more poetical I made my language, the more sternly practical she became.

Touch. Didn't she say anything about yellow moons? Oh, ho, ho!

de P. No, my Lord; she said she had joined the Amazon Club, and henceforth should regard men as the world's sub-

alterns.   She was so frigid that it was a positive relief when
the sash and Sir Meekly tumbled at our feet.

Touch.   Egad!   This is growing serious.   Something has
got to be done.

Sir H.   And I have begun to do it.   I have already sounded
Sir Meekly, and find him half disposed to revolt.   It only needs
our support to lead him to hang out the banner of rebellion, and
strike for liberty!

Touch.   Oh! magnificent! splendid! what fireworks we
shall have!   Oh, ho, ho, ho!

De P.   And you think he can actually be induced to brave
Lady Ironsides?

Sir H.   Sure of it, my dear sir; sure of it.   He only needs
a little backbone.

De P.   That's all an oyster needs to make it a fish.

Sir H.   But, in this case, it is in our power to furnish the
necessary amount.   Shall I have your co-operation?

De P.   With all my heart.

Touch.   And mine, and mine.   Sir Harry, you're a genius!
I compliment you.

(*Touchstone presents his snuff-box to Sir Harry; Sir Harry
presents his to de Portment; and de Portment presents his
to Touchstone.  All snuff simultaneously, and bow to each
other ceremoniously.*)

Touch.   Now let us consider.

De P.   How do you propose to operate?

Sir H.   Conjointly.

De P.   Hum.

Touch.   Old lady has a powerful hold!

Sir H.   Tremendous!

Touch.   And great strength of nerve.

De P.   Frightful!

Sir H.   But Sir Meekly's no fool.

Touch.   Well . . . N' no.   But . . .

De P.   Exactly!

Sir H.   Hum.

(*They look at each other, and snuff reflectively, as before.*)

De P.   What is to be done?

Sir H.   Let us go to him in a body, and stir him up.   It's
a matter of self-protection, I tell you.

Touch. Yes, you are right. The girls have no brains to squander on women's rights. Oh, ho, ho! I 'll back you, gentlemen, I 'll back you. (*aside.*) And I wager Mrs. Hector will think me more of an "old brute" than ever, before the fun is over. Ha!

De P. The poor gentleman has certainly cause for rebellion.

Sir H. And is quite ready to break his chains. Eh! (*looking off R.*) They are coming. We had best get to work.

Touch. By all means, by all means.

De P. (*looking off R.*) (*aside.*) I begin to think the old lady is not so partial to me, after all. She looks rather . . . indescribable! What can Sir Harry have meant?

(*Enter, R. 1 E., Lady Ironsides and Sappho. The gentlemen bow: the ladies regard them haughtily, and barely acknowledge the salute.*)

Sir H. (*aside.*) A thunderbolt is sunshine to Sappho!

(*Enter, L. U. E., Countess and Helena. The gentlemen pass up and bow. Helena regards them frigidly. Then exeunt, L., Touchstone, de Portment, and Sir Harry. The Countess and Helena come down.*)

Helena (*aside.*) So statuesque! But I am determined to take Lady Ironsides' advice.

Countess (*to Lady I.*) Are you ready to trump all the tricks, Lady Ironsides? You see we are semi-rural here, and usually get at our whist quite soon after dinner.

Lady I. Oh, I am quite ready to do the best I can with such hands as fate shall give me. As to trumping all the tricks, that's another matter. If one only didn't have to play with a man for partner; they are all so stupid.

Sappho. And so perfectly horrid! ah!

Countess. Goodness, Sappho! How vindictively you speak!

Lady I. She is entirely right, my Lady. I am glad to find in your niece so much good sound common sense. Indeed, both the young ladies have promised to take my advice in the matter of the men. I have expounded my views to them carefully, and I hope not without effect.

Sappho. Oh, no indeed! I see my folly. Why do you

5

know, aunt, I actually ranked men above horses, until dear
Lady Ironsides explained their true position to me.

COUNTESS. Good heavens!

SAPPHO. Think of it! The new system will change all
this absurd overestimation of men!

LADY I. Yes, indeed. Brute force has ruled the world long
enough. We propose, hereafter, that *mind* shall sway events;
the perfect, transcendent feminine mind.

SAPPHO. Hear, hear!

LADY I. We propose to relegate man to his proper place in
the economy of the universe . . .

HELENA. Hip hip . . .

SAPPHO. Hurrah!

HELENA. Tiger!

HELENA and SAPPHO. Ya–a–ah!

LADY I. We intend—we, the future women—that the lesser
male luminary shall revolve around our orbit, and take his
place, not in the van, but in the rear of our achievements!

HELENA and SAPPHO. Hear, hear!

LADY I. *We* shall make the laws; construe the laws; en-
force the laws . . .

HELENA. Blue laws! Hurrah!

LADY I. And march onward by right of our indomitable
will!

SAPPHO. We will! Hurrah!

LADY I. Onward and upward . . .

SAPPHO. Excel . . .

HELENA. Sior!

LADY I. The heaven-endowed rulers of the world!

SAPPHO. Hip hip . . .

HELENA. Hurrah! Tiger!

HELENA and SAPPHO. Ya–a–ah!

LADY I. Such is the destiny of woman!

COUNTESS. How is our navy to be manned?

LADY I. It won't be; it will be womaned.

HELENA. How very quaint!

SAPPHO. Hurrah!

LADY I. The Suffrage Association is about issuing a pamphlet which will sound the slogan of our liberties . . .
By the way, Sir Meekly was to have written about the matter

to-day. Will you send for him, please, my Lady. I'll inquire whether he has attended to it.

COUNTESS. Certainly.

(*Rings bell.*)

LADY I. When the nation reads that pamphlet . . .

COUNTESS (*aside.*) Yes; *when!*

LADY I. There will be a popular uprising.

(*Enter, L., Boggs.*)

COUNTESS. Inform Sir Meekly that Lady Ironsides desires to see him.

BOGGS. Yes, my Lady.

(*Exit, L., Boggs.*)

LADY I. Oh, 't will be a glorious change! Think of woman as the universal arbiter of peace and war!

SAPPHO. Especially war! I shall join the Royal Horse Guards. (*to Helena.*) Think of a squadron of side-saddles, dear.

HELENA. And the plumes! So mediæval, ah!

COUNTESS. Oh! what carnage we shall have, to be sure.

HELENA. And sha'n't some of us be postboys, too? I should so like to be a postboy. It has such a classical flavor . . .

SAPPHO. A mercurial profession.

HELENA. Yes, winged heels, and all that. Ah!

(*Enter, L., Boggs.*)

BOGGS. Sir Meekly sends his compliments, and says he's engaged at present.

LADY I. What! Engaged? Oh, he must have misunderstood! Tell Sir Meekly that Lady Ironsides desires his presence in the drawing-room. *Lady Ironsides*—you understand?

BOGGS. Yes, my Lady; I did, my Lady, but . . .

LADY I. His presence, *at once.*

BOGGS. Werry good, my Lady.

(*Exit, L., Boggs.*)

LADY I. He certainly could not have understood.

COUNTESS. And yet I was quite explicit. (*aside.*) I wonder if the little man has picked up a spirit. Ha, ha, ha!

HELENA. Under the new system, I suppose men will be

given *something* to do, won't they? It would never do to have them simply as ornaments.

SAPPHO.   They'd be sure to fail in that capacity.

LADY I.   Oh, I should not for a moment think of keeping men in idleness.   There are various occupations for which they are fitted.   But to have them in legislatures making laws for us is preposterous.   They can be assigned to many subordinate duties, but we must at all times exact instant obedience. Well?

*(Enter, L., Boggs.)*

BOGGS.   Beg pardon, my Lady, but Sir Meekly says that if your Ladyship's in a hurry, *you'll* have to come to *him*.   If not, he'll be coming to the drawing-room presently with the other gentlemen, and will be 'appy to 'ear your petition.

LADY I.   Hear my petition!   Oh, oh, ha!   And you mean to say that he gave you this message to carry to me?

BOGGS.   The same, my Lady.

COUNTESS *(aside.)*   A revolution!

LADY I.   To me!   Oh, this is . . . is . . . most extraordinary!   Most . . . most . . . unendurable.   *(aside.)*   "Other gentlemen," indeed.   Oh, I see the hand of Sir Harry Sang-froid in this!

COUNTESS.   That will do, Boggs.

*(Boggs bows and exit, L.)*

SAPPHO *(to Helena.)*   What can it mean?

HELENA *(to Sappho.)*   "Miching mallecho.   It means mischief!"

LADY I. *(aside.)*   "Petition," indeed!   Oh, wait till I see him; only wait!   *(aloud.)*   This is unexampled!

SAPPHO.   What is your Ladyship going to do about it?

LADY I.   Oh, I'll show you.   Sir Meekly has been tampered with.   He never would dare, of his own accord, to take such a step.

HELENA.   It's really awfully shocking, you know.

COUNTESS *(aside.)*   It looks to me like the approach of a crisis.

LADY I.   Such audacity must be checked.   *I* shall *check* it as soon as he comes.   *(aside.)*   "Petition," indeed!

COUNTESS. I am afraid your new disciples will lose faith, Lady Ironsides.

LADY I. Not when they see the disastrous results of such a violation of principle. Only wait, only wait.

SAPPHO (*to Helena.*) Do you think he can withstand her, sweet?

HELENA. Hardly; yet really I begin to doubt. But then how glorious to reign as she described; rulers of creation!

SAPPHO. Ah, yes! And Sir Harry! Ha! When I think of him I would like to be a . . . a . . . *cannibal!*

(*Enter, L. U. E., Sir Meekly, supported by Sir Harry, who in turn is supported by de Portment, and he in turn by Touchstone. Sir Meekly has head and foot bandaged, and patches of court-plaster on face; and is supported on two canes.*

LADY I. Oh! you have deigned to come, have you? And valiantly supported!

SIR M. Lady Ironsides, I come to d' declare to you thus p' publicly that . . . that . . .

SIR H. (*prompting him.*) I will no longer . . .

SIR M. I will no l' longer . . .

SIR H. (*as before.*) Be placed in the mortifying position . . .

SIR M. Be p' placed in the m' mortifying position of . . of . .

LADY I. Hold, sir! I understand this outrageous episode; I see through this revolt. It will not succeed, oh, ho! it will not succeed.

SIR M. Madam, I intend . . . I intend, Madam . . . I intend . . .

Sir H. (*as before.*) To assert my rights.

TOUCH. (*aside to Sir M.*) Spell it with a capital R. Hooray!

SIR M. To assert . . . to assert . . . (*aside.*) Oh heaven!

TOUCH. (*as before.*) Go it, Meekly, my boy!

SIR H. (*as before.*) My rights.

SIR M. My r' r' rights, madam.

LADY I. *Sir* Meekly!

SIR H. (*as before.*) I will no longer.

SIR M. I w' will no longer be . . . be . . .

DE P. (*aside to Sir M.*) Stick to it. Liberty or death!

SIR H. (*as before.*) Your slave!

SIR M. Y' your slave! I am . . . I am . . . I am . . .

HELENA (*aside to Sappho.*)  I believe he is.

SIR H. (*as before.*)  A man!

SIR M.  A–a–man, m' madam!

TOUCH. (*aside.*)  Hooray!

SAPPHO (*aside to Helena.*)  Heavens! sweet.  He says he 's a man!

SIR M.  I am . . . I am . . .

LADY I.  Sir Meekly, you 're a fool!

SIR M.  Enough, enough, I 'll . . . I 'll . . .

SIR H. (*as before.*)  Break this chain.

SIR M.  B' break this . . . (*aside.*) Oh, I 'm in an ague!

TOUCH. (*aside to Sir M.*)  Face the music, as the man said when he went to the dentist's.  Hooray!

SIR M.  This ch' chain.  I intend to . . .

DE P. (*aside.*)  Hear, hear!

SIR H. (*as before.*)  Strike for liberty!

SIR M.  S' strike for lib–lib–liberty!

LADY I.  *Sir* Meekly, are you mad?

TOUCH.  By Mars!  *I'm getting* mad!

LADY I.  Cease this foolery, instantly . . .

SIR M.  No madam, I will be free!  I will be . . . be . .

SIR H. (*as before.*)  Master.

SIR M.  I will be.  (*aside.*) Oh, dear!

SIR H. (*as before.*)  Master.

SIR M.  M' master!

(*Lady I., Helena, and Sappho scream.  Helena and Sappho lean against Lady I. for support.*)

SIR H.  Bravo!

LADY I.  *Sir* Meekly.  How *dare* you?

SIR M.  I will . . . I will . . . (*aside.*) Oh, it 's no use. Her eye is on me.  I 'm gone!  I 'm gone!

LADY I.  Enough of this.  Let me tell you that I comprehend this insolence.  You, sir (*to Sir H.*), are at the bottom of it; you who dared to write me a love-letter . . .

SIR H.  On my honor, madam, I never did.

LADY I.  What!

SIR H.  The tender epistle which you received was addressed to Lady Sappho.

SAPPHO.  Oh!  To *me?*  (*aside.*) Oh, I don't feel nearly so much like a cannibal as I did.

LADY I. This is extraordinary.

COUNTESS (*aside*). Lady Ironsides' ranks are broken. Her troops are going to desert.

SIR H. The whole business was a blunder. You received the letter intended for Sappho, while she . . .

TOUCH. Received the blowing-up intended for my rascally tailor. Oh, ho, ho, ho!

SAPPHO (*aside.*) Oh, happiness!

(*Sappho runs to Sir Harry, and lays her head on his shoulder.*)

LADY I. What! You recant, weakling?

SAPPHO (*aside.*) I think my pose is rather Greek.

HELENA (*aside.*) Dear me!

DE P. May I not hope to share in the recantation?

HELENA (*aside.*) He is *very* statuesque. (*aloud.*) Lady Ironsides, I leave "Woman's Vengeance," to you.

(*Helena runs to de Portment, and lays her head on his shoulder.*)

TOUCH. Osage and orange-blossoms! What a go! Oh, ho, ho, ho!

SIR M. I f' feel like a f' fish out of water.

(*Sir Meekly hobbles to Lady Ironsides, and lays his head on her shoulder affectedly.*)

LADY I. Pah!

(*General merriment.*)

COUNTESS. I fear, my dear Lady Ironsides, that you must seek for recruits elsewhere. You likewise, Sir Harry.

SIR H. Madam, I am quite satisfied with the exchange of prisoners.

DE P. And I desire an armistice.

(*Enter, L. U. E., Boggs.*)

BOGGS. My Lord, the whist-tables are placed.

TOUCH. Good. Then choose your partners.

COUNTESS (*laughing.*) Everybody seems to have done that pretty effectually already.

TOUCH. Except . . .

(*He holds out his hand to Countess.*)

COUNTESS. Oh, no; exceptions ever prove the rule.
(*She goes to Touchstone.*)

TOUCH. Or did, my Lady, when *I* went to school.

DE P. I have an idea!

SIR H. What, thou gay deceiver?
(*aside.*) Two-ideas in a day—I fear brain fever!

DE P. Let 's play our whist to tune of wedding-bells.

LADY I. 'Gainst *such* an idea all my sense rebels.

TOUCH. (*aside.*) Not much of a rebellion! Ha, ha, ha!

DE P. What say *you*, Helena?

HELENA. Oh, ask papa!

SIR H. And *you*, fair Sappho?

SAPPHO. Ah, excuse were vain!
(*aside.*) I 'll wear white satin with a velvet train.

BOGGS (*aside, at back.*) It looks as if we 'd have a weddin'
weekly.

SIR M. (*to Lady I.*) D' dear L' Lady, do you l' love your
little M' Meekly?

LADY I. Love 's but a word.

COUNTESS. One word sets all things right.

SIR H. I think we owe our friends (*indicating audience*)
*two* words :

ALL (*to audience.*) Good night.

BOGGS.
*

SIR MEEKLY.               SAPPHO.
*                            *

LADY IRONSIDES.           SIR HARRY.
*                            *

TOUCHSTONE.               HELENA.
*                            *

COUNTESS.                 DE PORTMENT.
*                            *

## CURTAIN.